UNDERCOVER ANIMALS

Printed exclusively for Baker and Taylor

First published in Great Britain in 2019 by Mortimer Children's Limited, an imprint of Welbeck Publishing Group, 20 Mortimer Street, London W1T 3JW.

This edition published in the United States in 2021 by Mortimer Children's Limited, an imprint of the Welbeck Publishing Group.

ISBN: 978-1-83935-107-5

Printed in Dongguan, China
9 8 7 6 5 4 3 2 1

Executive Editor: Bryony Davies
Editor: Jennie Roman
Art Editor: Deborah Vickers
Designer: Dani Lurie
Picture Research: Paul Langan

The publishers would like to thank the following sources for their kind permission to reproduce the pictures in this book. Key: T=top, B=bottom, L=left, R=right & BKG=background.

Alamy: /Avalon/Photoshot Licence: 12TL; /Dennis Cox: 27; /David Fleetham: 32TR; /Urs Hauenstein: 20BR; /imageBROKER: 26B, 29; /Minden Pictures: 10TL, 10BR; /National Geographic Image Collectuion: 26T; /Stuart Robertson: 28BR; /Kumar Sriskandan: 9; /Marli Wakeling: 31; /Margaret Welby: 30BR

Getty Images: /Philippe Royer/Gamma-Rapho: 7; /Steve Winter: 5

Shutterstock: /Aaronejbull87: 14TL; /AlenaHK: 3; /AndreAnita: 22TL; /Jiri Balek: 18TL; /Sourabh Bharti: 6BR; /blue-sea.cz: 13; /Ryan M Bolton: 18BR; /Mark Brandon: 24TR; /bulentevren: 4BKG; /Jan Bures: 8BR; /phichet chalyabin: 23; /Divelvanov: 32BL; /Nico Faramaz: 14BR; /Karen Grigoryan: 28TL; /hlopex: 22BR; /Ingo L: 4BL; /Sebastian Janicki: 16BL; /Kjersti Joergensen: 20TL; /Olaf Kruger/imageBROKER: 8TL; /Lensalot: 6TL; /Nuk2013: 24BL; /Matee Nuserm: 2BR; /Ekkapan Poddamrong: 25; /Ondrej Prosicky: 21; /zaidi razak: 11, 16TR; /reptiles4all: 15; /Damian Ryszawy: 17; /Anna Veselova: 1; /Peter Wey: 30TL; /Pong Wira: 12BR; /Milan Zygmunt: 2BKG, 19

Every effort has been made to acknowledge correctly and contact the source and/or copyright holder of each picture, and Welbeck Publishing Limited apologizes for any unintentional errors or omissions that will be corrected in future editions of this book.

UNDERCOVER
ANIMALS

WRITTEN BY
CAMILLA DE
LA BÉDOYÈRE

MORTIMER

Are you as sharp-eyed as an eagle and good at spotting clues? If the answer is "yes," you will make a great animal detective!

Look carefully inside these pages and you will find sneaky spiders, shape-shifting sea creatures, and animals that are so good at hiding they are almost invisible. Some creatures don't bother to hide—they simply pretend to be something else instead!

Find out if these masters of disguise are using their super skills to stay out of trouble, or if they are hiding so they can get close to another animal before launching a surprise attack. There's plenty to discover so keep your eyes peeled!

WHERE AM I?

Who's hiding in the long grass? This stripy hunter silently prowls through the forest.

TERRIBLE TIGER!

Tigers usually hunt when the sun goes down. They creep up on their prey without being seen, and can kill animals with just one bite to the back of the neck.

The dark stripes on a tiger's fur help it to vanish in the shadows.

WOW!
TIGERS ARE SO STRONG THEY SOMETIMES ATTACK CROCODILES!

MOST CATS HATE WATER BUT TIGERS LOVE IT.

WHAT AM I?

This scaly-skinned reptile is hiding in the trees, keeping an eye out for danger!

INCREDIBLE CHAMELEON!

Chameleons can move each of their eyes separately. They can also twirl them around!

Female panther chameleons are often shy, and like to hide. But this male wears a rainbow of color! He can switch his skin from dull to bright in seconds to warn other chameleons to stay away.

WOW!

WHEN A CHAMELEON SLEEPS, ITS SKIN LOSES SOME OF ITS COLOR.

CAN YOU SEE ME?

What can you spy in the seaweed? This master of disguise only lives in the shallow seas around Australia.

FREAKY FISH!

This bizarre fish is a leafy sea dragon, a close cousin of the seahorse. It's perfectly camouflaged to hide in the seaweed where it lives, feeding on tiny shrimp.

WOW!

SEA DRAGONS AND SEAHORSES ARE NOT STRONG SWIMMERS.

Male sea dragons look after the eggs. They keep them under their tail until they are ready to hatch.

WHO'S HIDING HERE?

What eight-legged beast is lurking beneath a trapdoor? Beware this mini-monster!

SCARY SPIDER!

Trapdoor spiders are great at hiding. They dig a burrow and cover the entrance with a door. When a bug walks past, the spider leaps out and grabs it!

Trapdoor spiders kill their prey by biting them and injecting venom.

WOW!

THESE SPIDERS CAN DELIVER A NASTY BITE, BUT THEY ARE NOT DEADLY TO PEOPLE-JUST BUGS!

WHAT AM I?

The patterns on this animal's
back help it to hide on the seabed.
Do you know what it is?

SNEAKY SHARK!

This is a wobbegong shark and it spends the day snoozing on the floor of the shallow sea. At night it sneaks up on crabs and lobsters and sucks them into its mouth.

The strange tassels that grow on the shark's skin help it blend into the background.

WOBBEGONGS BELONG TO A FAMILY OF FISH CALLED CARPET SHARKS BECAUSE THEY LIE ON THE SEABED.

HOW DO I HUNT?

This looks like a beautiful flower, but it's a deadly predator that tricks its way to hunting success.

BEAUTIFUL BUG!

Orchid mantises look like flowers to trick bugs into coming close. Then they launch an attack with lightning speed to kill their prey.

Bugs think they are visiting a flower to feast on the petals or nectar. Surprise!

MANTISES GRAB BUGS IN THEIR FRONT LEGS, THEN CRUNCH THEM WITH POWERFUL JAWS.

"LEAF" ME ALONE!

Pretending to be a leaf is a good disguise if you live in a tree. What type of animal is this?

GORGEOUS GECKO!

A gecko is a lizard that lives in trees. Many geckos are green, but leaf-tailed geckos go one step farther and take on the shape of a plant!

Birds and snakes eat geckos, so it's a good idea to hide from view.

THIS LEAF-TAILED GECKO IS CAMOUFLAGED TO LOOK LIKE MOSS.

WHO GROWS GREEN?

Who is hairy, slow, and lives upside down?
This rain forest animal even turns green!

SLEEPY SLOTH!

Three-toed sloths use their long claws to hang from branches.

Tiny green plants grow in their fur. This makes it hard for jaguars and other predators to find them in the treetops!

WOW!

SLOTHS ARE SOME OF THE WORLD'S SLOWEST ANIMALS AND THEY SLEEP FOR 20 HOURS A DAY!

BABY SLOTHS CLING TIGHTLY TO MOM.

WHO IS HIDING IN THE SNOW?

This white animal spends the winter fast asleep in a snow den, but she has a surprise waiting for you!

CUTE BEAR CUBS!

A polar bear mom gives birth to her cubs in a den. In the spring it's time for them to come out and play!

White fur is perfect camouflage in the snow.

POLAR BEARS HUNT SEALS IN THE ARCTIC. THEIR THICK FUR KEEPS THEM WARM.

WHO'S PRETENDING TO BE A LEAF?

When an animal pretends to be something else, it's called a mimic, and this is one of nature's best mimics!

LOVELY LEAF INSECT!

Leaf insects have a flat, broad body, and even have marks that look like leaf veins.

Insects are food for many other animals, so it's no wonder that some of them make a big effort to stay safe. Leaf insects are such perfect mimics they even fool their mates!

THEY CAN SHAKE LIKE LEAVES BLOWING IN THE WIND!

WHO'S DRESSING UP?

Some animals like to decorate themselves, just like we do! This fashion-loving ocean creature has an eye for color.

CLEVER DECORATOR CRAB!

Some crabs decorate their shells with stones, seaweed, or sponges to hide or stay safe. They have hooked hairs on their shells that keep the decorations in place.

Most decorator crabs live in shallow ocean waters.

SOME DECORATOR CRABS WEAR STINGING SEA ANEMONES TO KEEP PREDATORS AWAY.

WHO'S KEEPING AN EYE ON YOU?

Some eyes are for seeing, but others are for being seen.
Which mystery animal owns these eyes?

BIG-EYED OWL BUTTERFLY!

Owl butterflies have huge eye-spots that trick predators into thinking they are owls.

The eye-shaped patterns on a butterfly's wings are called eye-spots. When the butterfly flaps its wings, the "eyes" flash and scare predators away.

A BUTTERFLY'S REAL EYES ARE ON ITS HEAD. LIKE ALL INSECTS, BUTTERFLIES CAN'T SEE THE COLOR RED.

WHO IS CHANGING COLOR?

A leopard can't change its spots, but this animal can change its color with the seasons.

BOUNCY MOUNTAIN HARE!

Mountain hares live in cool northern places where the winters are long and snowy. Their brown fur turns white for the winter!

Hares are members of the rabbit family.

WOW!
MOST HARES HAVE LONGER EARS THAN RABBITS.

They have long legs for leaping and running fast.

IN THE SPRING A HARE'S FUR TURNS BROWN SO IT'S ALWAYS PERFECTLY CAMOUFLAGED.

WHO IS CHANGING SHAPE?

This is a soft-bodied shape-shifter with some surprising tricks up its eight sleeves!

MIMIC OCTOPUS!

Octopuses can change color to blend in with their surroundings, but this octopus can also change its shape. It pretends to be a sea snake, coral, or a fish!

Mimic octopuses live in warm shallow ocean waters.

OCTOPUSES DON'T HAVE BONES, BUT THEIR EIGHT ARMS ARE COVERED IN STRONG SUCKERS.